Greetings From
CLEARWATER
FLORIDA

Greetings From
CLEARWATER
FLORIDA

Greetings From
CLEARWATER
FLORIDA

Greetings From
CLEARWATER
FLORIDA

Greetings From
CLEARWATER
FLORIDA

Greetings From
CLEARWATER
FLORIDA

Greetings From
CLEARWATER
FLORIDA

Greetings From
CLEARWATER
FLORIDA

Greetings From
CLEARWATER
FLORIDA

Greetings From
CLEARWATER
FLORIDA

Greetings From
CLEARWATER
FLORIDA

Greetings From
CLEARWATER
FLORIDA

Greetings From
CLEARWATER
FLORIDA

Greetings From
CLEARWATER
FLORIDA

Greetings From
CLEARWATER
FLORIDA

Greetings From
CLEARWATER
FLORIDA

Greetings From
CLEARWATER
FLORIDA

Greetings From
CLEARWATER
FLORIDA

Greetings From
CLEARWATER
FLORIDA

Greetings From
CLEARWATER
FLORIDA

Greetings From
CLEARWATER
FLORIDA

Greetings From
CLEARWATER
FLORIDA

Greetings From
CLEARWATER
FLORIDA

Greetings From
CLEARWATER
FLORIDA

Greetings From
CLEARWATER
FLORIDA

Greetings From
CLEARWATER
FLORIDA

Greetings From
CLEARWATER
FLORIDA

Greetings From
CLEARWATER
FLORIDA

Greetings From
CLEARWATER
FLORIDA

Greetings From
CLEARWATER
FLORIDA

Greetings From
CLEARWATER
FLORIDA

Greetings From
CLEARWATER
FLORIDA

Greetings From
CLEARWATER
FLORIDA

Greetings From
CLEARWATER
FLORIDA

Greetings From
CLEARWATER
FLORIDA

Greetings From
CLEARWATER
FLORIDA

Greetings From
CLEARWATER
FLORIDA

Greetings From
CLEARWATER
FLORIDA

Greetings From
CLEARWATER
FLORIDA

Greetings From
CLEARWATER
FLORIDA

Greetings From
CLEARWATER
FLORIDA

Greetings From
CLEARWATER
FLORIDA

Greetings From
CLEARWATER
FLORIDA

Greetings From
CLEARWATER
FLORIDA

Greetings From
CLEARWATER
FLORIDA

Greetings From
CLEARWATER
FLORIDA

Greetings From
CLEARWATER
FLORIDA

Greetings From
CLEARWATER
FLORIDA

Greetings From
CLEARWATER
FLORIDA

Greetings From
CLEARWATER
FLORIDA

Greetings From
CLEARWATER
FLORIDA

Greetings From
CLEARWATER
FLORIDA

Greetings From
CLEARWATER
FLORIDA

Greetings From
CLEARWATER
FLORIDA

Greetings From
CLEARWATER
FLORIDA

Greetings From
CLEARWATER
FLORIDA

Greetings From
CLEARWATER
FLORIDA

Greetings From
CLEARWATER
FLORIDA

Greetings From
CLEARWATER
FLORIDA

Greetings From
CLEARWATER
FLORIDA

Greetings From
CLEARWATER
FLORIDA

Greetings From
CLEARWATER
FLORIDA

Greetings From
CLEARWATER
FLORIDA

Greetings From
CLEARWATER
FLORIDA

Greetings From
CLEARWATER
FLORIDA

Greetings From
CLEARWATER
FLORIDA

Greetings From
CLEARWATER
FLORIDA

Greetings From
CLEARWATER
FLORIDA

Greetings From
CLEARWATER
FLORIDA

Greetings From
CLEARWATER
FLORIDA

Greetings From
CLEARWATER
FLORIDA

Greetings From
CLEARWATER
FLORIDA

Greetings From
CLEARWATER
FLORIDA

Greetings From
CLEARWATER
FLORIDA

Greetings From
CLEARWATER
FLORIDA

Printed in the USA
CPSIA information can be obtained
at www.ICGtesting.com
LVHW040220190524
780684LV00017B/60

9 798385 409709